Pebble® Plus

T0100914

Cycles of Nature

The Water Cycle

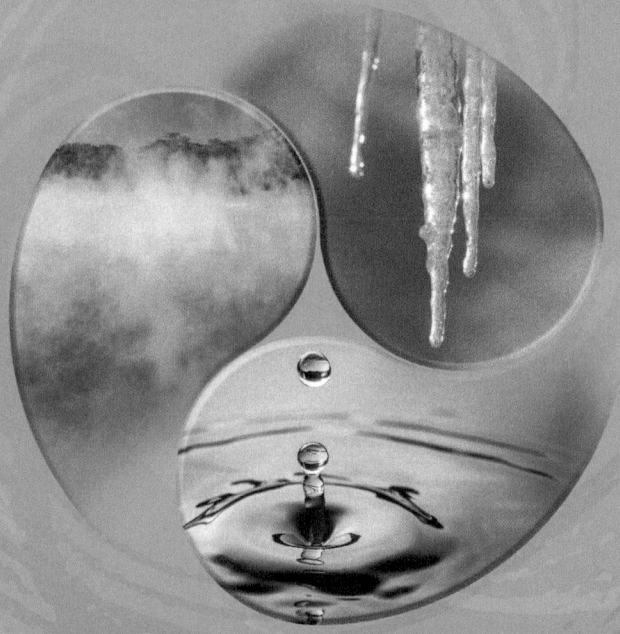

by Catherine Ipcizade

Consultant: Dr. Sandra F. Mather, Professor Emerita
Department of Earth and Space Sciences
West Chester University, West Chester, Pa.

PEBBLE
a capstone imprint

Pebble Plus is published by Pebble
1710 Roe Crest Drive, North Mankato, Minnesota 56003
capstonepub.com

Copyright © 2019 by Pebble, a Capstone imprint. All rights reserved. No part of this publication may be reproduced in whole or in part, or stored in a retrieval system, or transmitted in any form or by any means, electronic, mechanical, photocopying, recording, or otherwise, without written permission of the publisher.

Library of Congress Cataloging-in-Publication Data
Names: Ipcizade, Catherine, author.
Title: The water cycle : a 4D book / by Catherine Ipcizade.
Description: North Mankato, Minnesota : Pebble, [2019] | Series: Pebble plus. Cycles of nature | Audience: Ages 4–8.
Identifiers: LCCN 2018002966 (print) | LCCN 2018021552 (ebook) | ISBN 9781977100474 (eBook PDF) | ISBN 9781977100399 (hardcover) | ISBN 9781977100436 (pbk.)
Subjects: LCSH: Hydrologic cycle—Juvenile literature. | Rain and rainfall—Juvenile literature. | Water—Juvenile literature.
Classification: LCC GB848 (ebook) | LCC GB848 .I63 2019 (print) | DDC 551.48—dc23
LC record available at https://lccn.loc.gov/2018002966

Summary: Lakes evaporate. Clouds form from condensation. Rain falls and fills rivers and lakes. Soak up facts about the water cycle and why we need to keep water clean.

Editorial Credits
Emily Raij, editor; Charmaine Whitman, designer;
Eric Gohl, media researcher; Kris Wilfahrt, production specialist

Image Credits
Newscom: Blend Images/Ariel Skelley, 21; Shutterstock: aekikuis, 5, Alexey Osokin, cover (left), 1 (left), Eakachai Leesin, 17, FenlioQ, 7, Firstyahoo, cover (bottom), 1 (bottom), Kuzmenko Viktoria, 10, Neirfy, 15, Ostariyanov, 9, pixy_nook, 11, Rich Carey, 19, Serkan Senturk, 13, Zhivka Kalinkova, cover (right), 1 (right)
Design Elements: Shutterstock

Note to Parents and Teachers

The Cycles of Nature set supports the national science standards related to patterns in the natural world. This book describes and illustrates the water cycle. The images support early readers in understanding the text. The repetition of words and phrases helps early readers learn new words. This book also introduces early readers to subject-specific vocabulary words, which are defined in the Glossary section. Early readers may need assistance to read some words and to use the Table of Contents, Glossary, Read More, Internet Sites, Critical Thinking Questions, and Index sections of the book.

Printed in the United States 5961

Table of Contents

The Water Cycle 4

Liquid to Gas 6

Clouds at Work 10

From Water to Ice 14

People and Water 16

Glossary 22

Read More 23

Critical Thinking Questions 23

Index 24

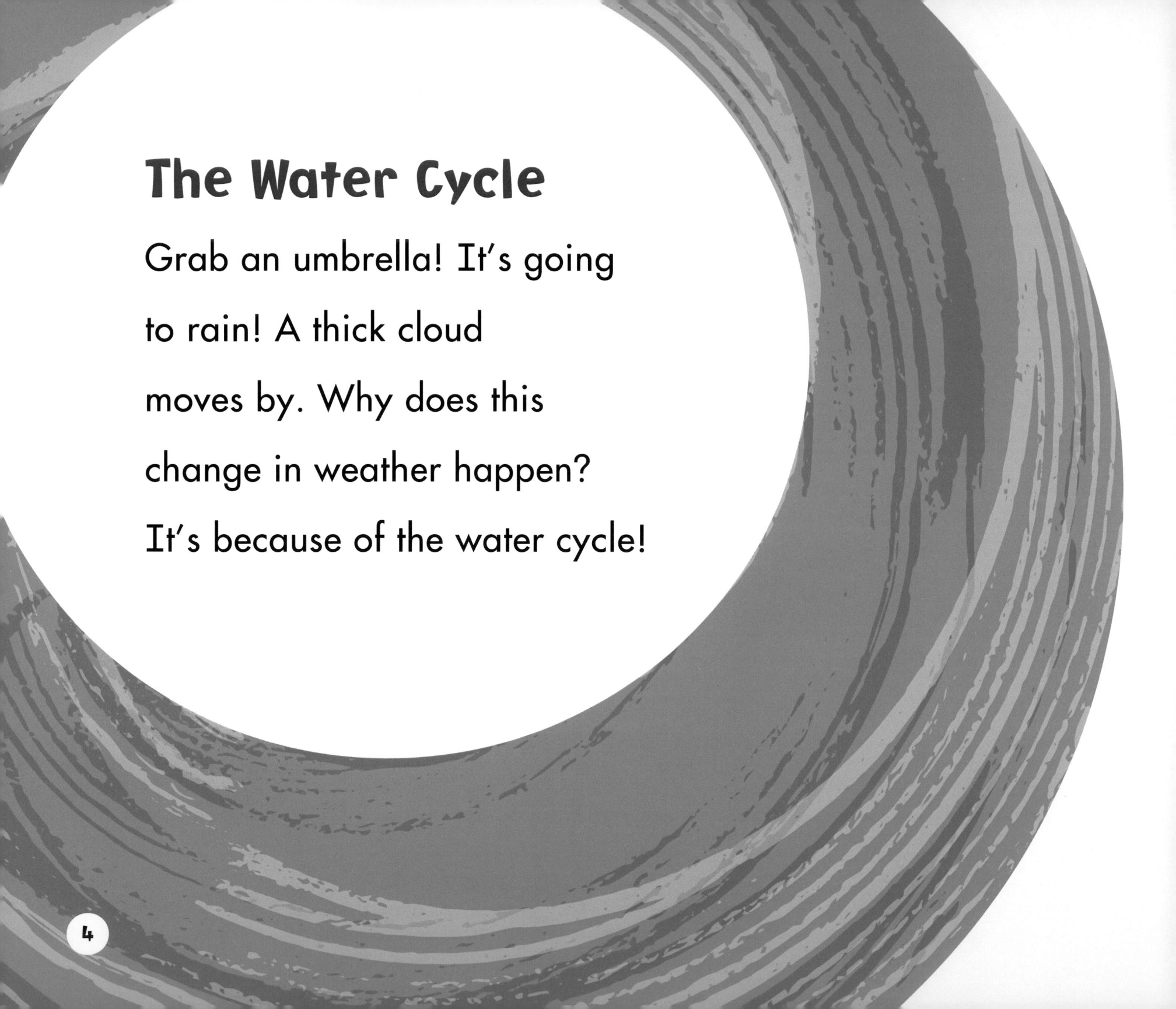

The Water Cycle

Grab an umbrella! It's going to rain! A thick cloud moves by. Why does this change in weather happen? It's because of the water cycle!

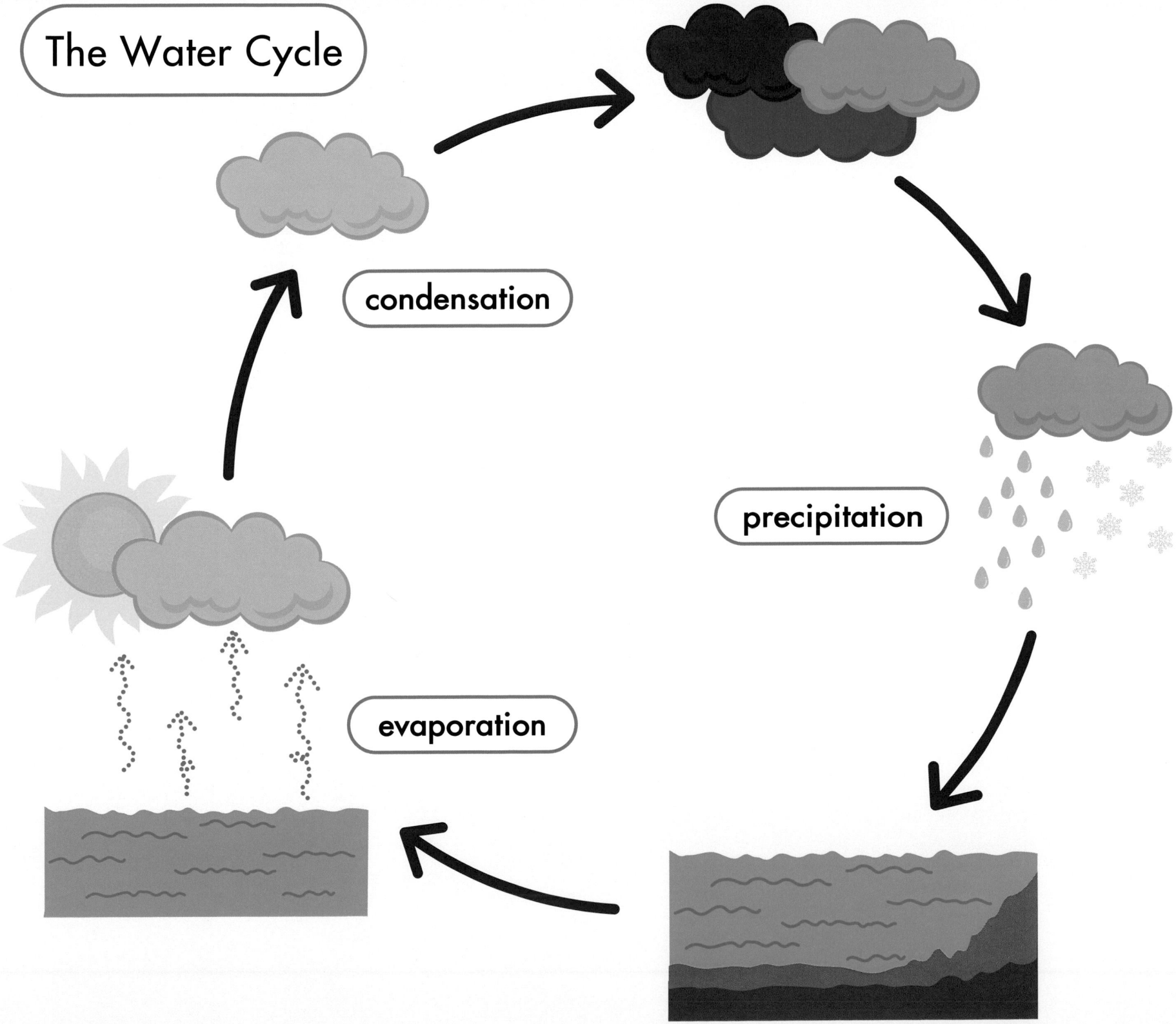
The Water Cycle
condensation
precipitation
evaporation

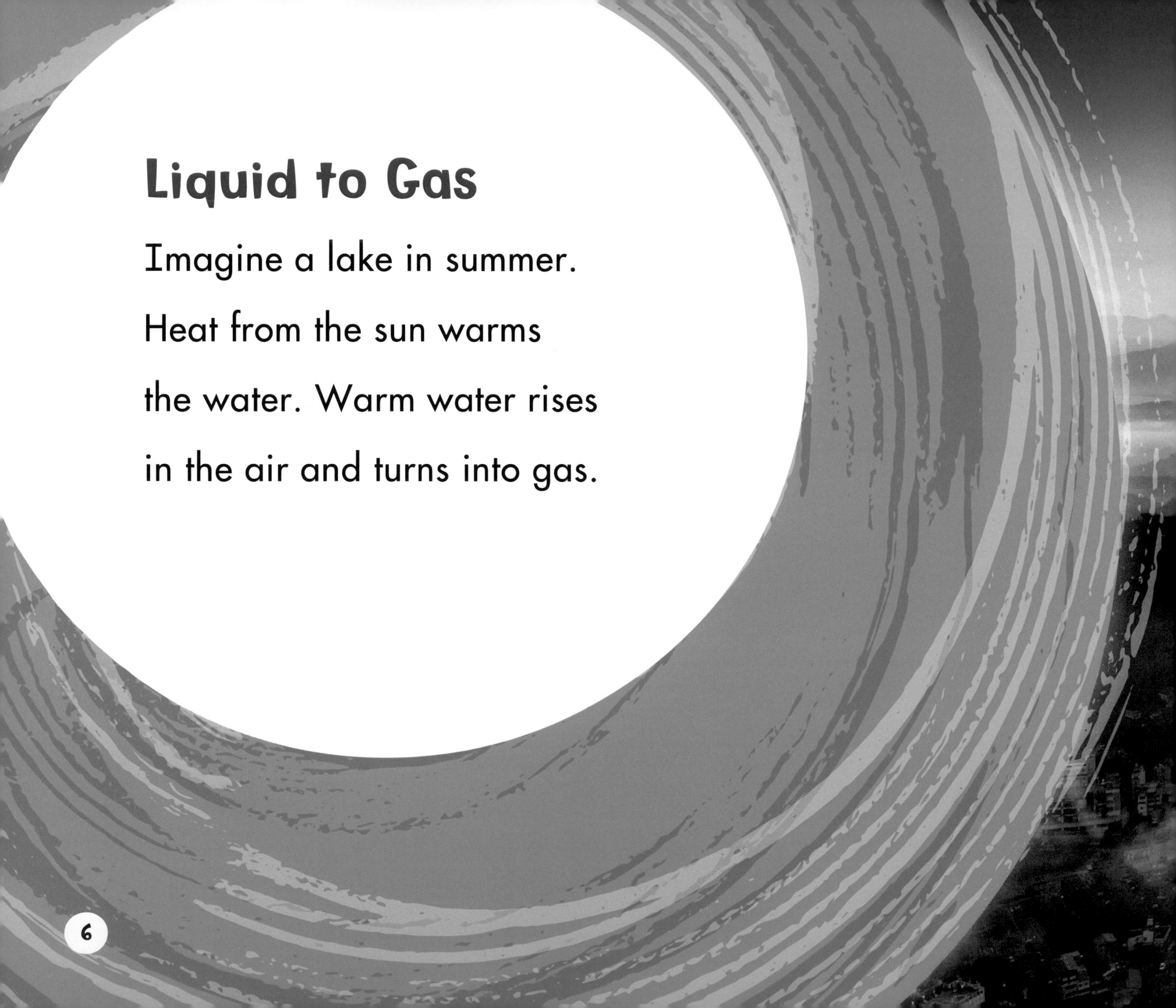

Liquid to Gas

Imagine a lake in summer. Heat from the sun warms the water. Warm water rises in the air and turns into gas.

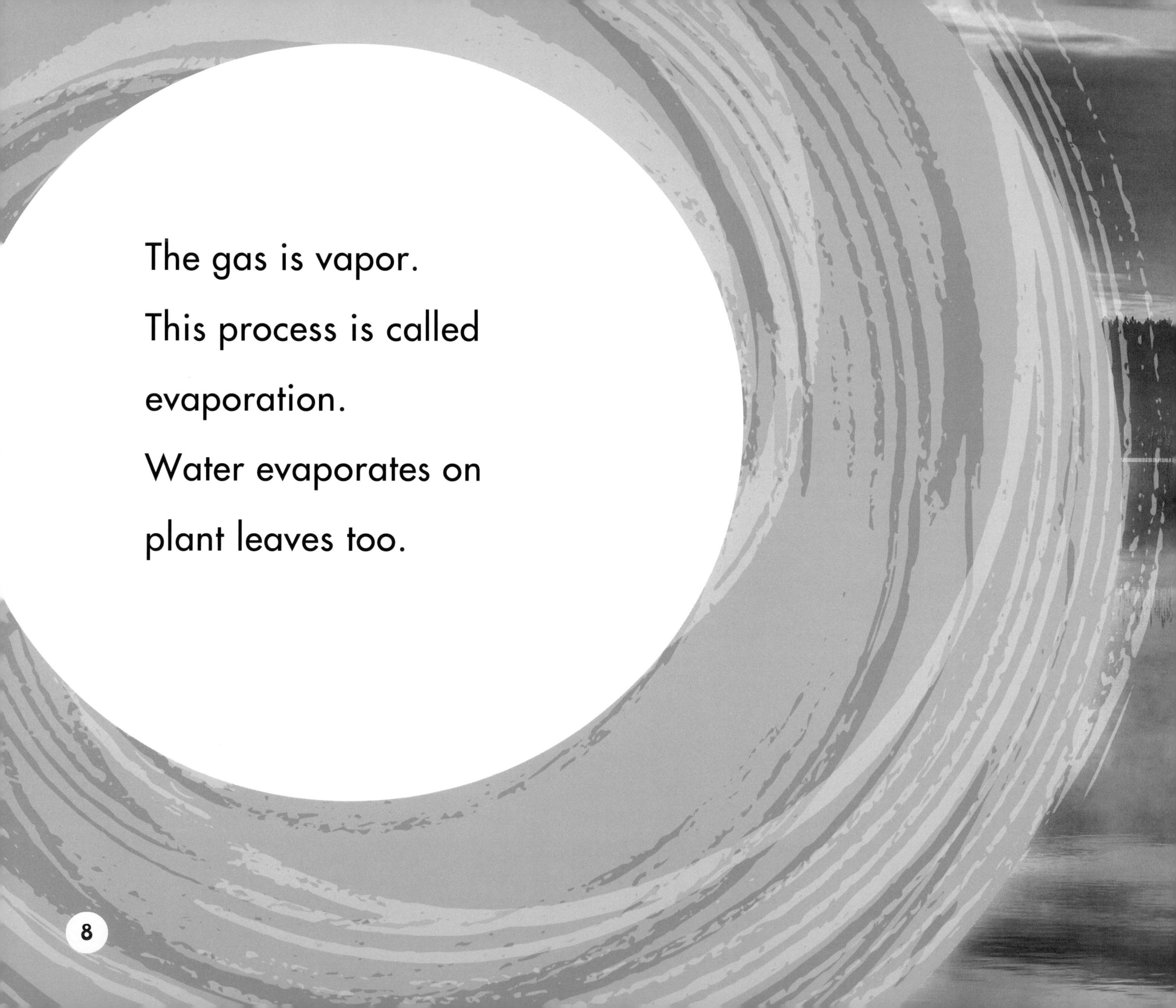

The gas is vapor.
This process is called
evaporation.
Water evaporates on
plant leaves too.

Clouds at Work

Vapor from lakes and oceans cools. It turns into tiny water droplets. This is called condensation, which makes clouds or dew.

Clouds are made of water droplets. The droplets become too heavy. That's when rain or snow falls. This is called precipitation.

precipitation

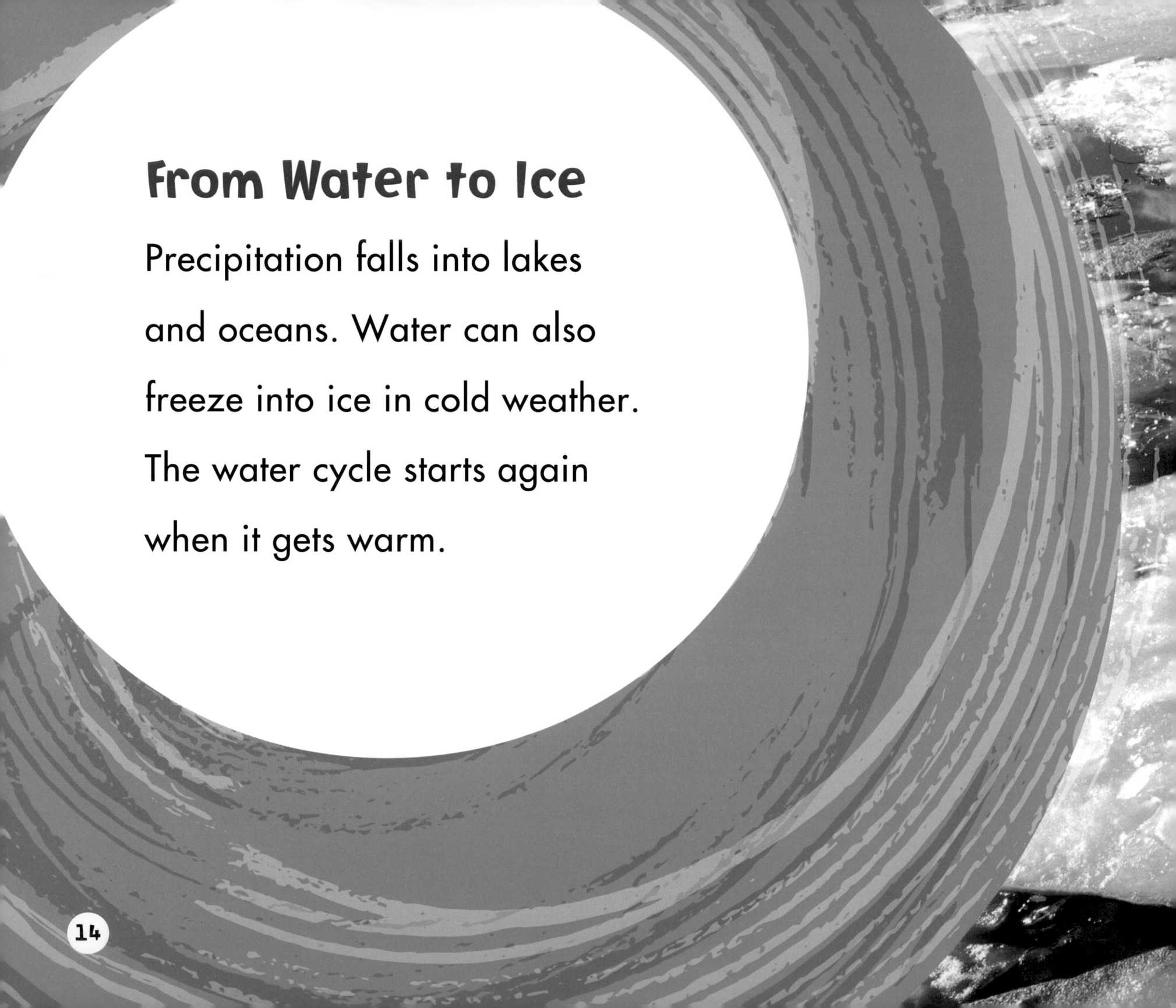

From Water to Ice

Precipitation falls into lakes and oceans. Water can also freeze into ice in cold weather. The water cycle starts again when it gets warm.

People and Water

The water cycle has repeated for billions of years. Our water has been on Earth a long time. We drink the same water the first people on Earth drank!

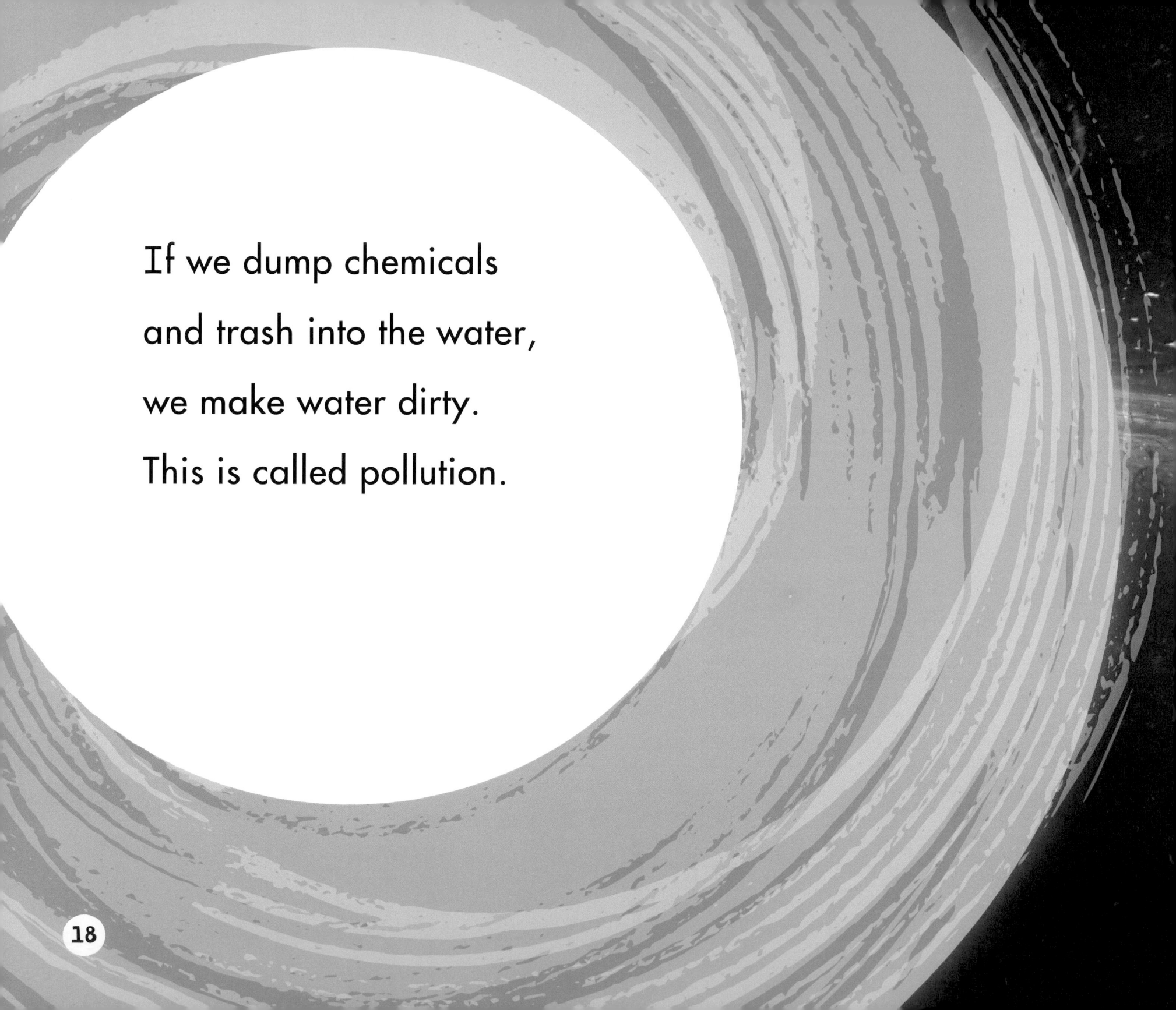

If we dump chemicals
and trash into the water,
we make water dirty.
This is called pollution.

Dirty water is dangerous to drink. It can change what lives and grows in places too. We need to work to keep our water clean.

VOLUNTEER

Glossary

condensation—changing from a gas to a liquid

dew—small water droplets that collect overnight on outside surfaces, such as plant leaves

evaporation—changing from a liquid to a gas

pollution—materials that hurt Earth's water, air, and land

precipitation—water that falls from clouds to Earth's surface; precipitation can be rain, hail, sleet, or snow.

vapor—a gas made from a liquid or a solid

weather—the condition outdoors at a certain time and place; weather changes with each season.

Read More

Maloof, Torrey. *Water Cycle.* Science Readers: Content and Literacy. Huntington Beach, Calif.: Teacher Created Materials, 2015.

Olien, Rebecca. *The Water Cycle at Work.* Water in Our World. North Mankato, Minn.: Capstone Press, 2016.

Stewart, Melissa. *Water.* National Geographic Readers. Washington, D.C.: National Geographic Children's Books, 2014.

Critical Thinking Questions

1. Why doesn't water evaporate as much during the winter?
2. Why does it rain?
3. How can people help keep water clean?

Index

clouds, 4, 10, 12
condensation, 10
dew, 10
evaporation, 8
gas, 6, 8
ice, 14
liquid, 6
pollution, 18
precipitation, 12, 14
rain, 4, 12
snow, 12
sun, 6
vapor, 8, 10
weather, 4, 14